BOOK BANS

BOOK BANS

Reading Under Siege

Sally McGraw

LERNER PUBLICATIONS ◆ MINNEAPOLIS

To my elementary school reading and language arts teacher, Ellen Esrick, who taught me that reading is a window to the world.

Lerner Publications Company
An imprint of Lerner Publishing Group, Inc.
241 First Avenue North
Minneapolis, MN 55401 USA

For reading levels and more information, look up this title at www.lernerbooks.com.

Main body text set in ITC Garamond Std Book.
Typeface provided by Adobe Systems.

Editor: Anne E. Hill **Designer:** Athena Currier

Library of Congress Cataloging-in-Publication Data

Names: McGraw, Sally author
Title: Book bans : reading under siege / Sally McGraw.
Description: Minneapolis : Lerner Publications, [2026] | Series: Gateway headlines | Includes bibliographical references and index | Audience term: juvenile | Audience term: Preteens | Audience term: Teenagers | Audience: Ages 9–14 | Audience: Grades 4–6 | Summary: "Book bans are a topic that has taken the US by storm. Readers delve into the matter in this close-up examination of the controversies and consequences surrounding challenged and banned books in libraries and schools"— Provided by publisher
Identifiers: LCCN 2024039668 (print) | LCCN 2024039669 (ebook) | ISBN 9798765684146 paperback | ISBN 9798765669396 library binding | ISBN 9798765677612 epub
Subjects: LCSH: Libraries—Censorship—United States—Juvenile literature | Intellectual freedom—United States—Juvenile literature | Prohibited books—United States—Juvenile literature | Challenged books—United States—Juvenile literature | Children—Books and reading—United States—Juvenile literature | Teenagers—Books and reading—United States—Juvenile literature
Classification: LCC Z711.4 .M316 2026 (print) | LCC Z711.4 (ebook) | DDC 098/.10973—dc23/eng/20241204

LC record available at https://lccn.loc.gov/2024039668
LC ebook record available at https://lccn.loc.gov/2024039669

Manufactured in the United States of America
1-1011881-53910-2/14/2025

Table of Contents

Libraries as Battlegrounds ____________ 9

What Exactly Is a Book Ban? ____________ 14

Fear of Ideas ____________ 16

When Governments Step In ____________ 21

Censorship ____________ 26

Books at Libraries vs. Books at Schools ____ 32

Legal Loopholes ____________ 37

Pushing Back against Bans ____________ 39

Important Dates ____________ 42

Source Notes ____________ 44

Selected Bibliography ____________ 45

Learn More ____________ 46

Index ____________ 47

The entrance to the Campbell County Courthouse in Gillette, Wyoming

In the town of Gillette, Wyoming, a librarian named Terri Lesley was under attack. Lesley had worked in the Campbell County Public Library for twenty-seven years, including eleven years as its director. Lesley believed in the importance of providing access to a wide range of books for everyone in her community.

However, throughout 2021 and 2022, she was asked to remove books on LGBTQIA+ topics from the library's collection. She refused. "I believe the community is harmed by not having access to a wide variety of information," Lesley told a reporter. "Public libraries are for everyone. Our collection should serve all citizens of the community." She stood up for her beliefs for two years. After a long battle with the library board, Lesley was fired from her job in July 2023.

Lesley's story is not unique. Librarians all over the United States are being pressured to remove books that some people find controversial. Librarians in Michigan, Texas, Colorado, Idaho, and many other states have been fired for refusing to remove certain books from their shelves. Some libraries have received threats of violence. Others have lost their funding because of the books and educational programs they offer. Librarians have even received death threats for protecting certain books.

In 2023 the American Library Association (ALA) reported that 4,240 different books were targeted for removal from schools and libraries. That's a 65 percent increase from the previous year. Many of these books cover topics related to race, gender, and sexuality. Books that people in Lesley's community challenged included *Gender Queer* by Maia Kobabe, *Lawn Boy* by Jonathan

Titles on LGBTQIA+ topics, such as these books on display at The New York Public Library's Stavros Niarchos Foundation Library, are among the most frequently banned.

Evison, and *This Book Is Gay* by Juno Dawson. All of these books tell LGBTQIA+ stories.

Librarians such as Lesley play an important role in defending the freedom to read. They work hard to make sure that libraries offer a variety of books for everyone. When a book is challenged, librarians are often forced to defend the book. They must explain why it should stay on the shelves. Some librarians are even willing to lose their jobs to stand up against book bans. Banning books is not new. But the practice has become more widespread in recent years.

Libraries as Battlegrounds

Imagine walking into your local library and finding empty shelves where your favorite books used to be. Or going to look for a book about a sensitive topic and finding nothing. Library users across the United States are finding themselves in these situations.

One reason for the increase in book bans is political division. People have differing ideas about how institutions such as libraries should be run. Some groups believe certain topics or ideas should not be represented in libraries.

Many of these groups believe books about sexuality and race should not be available to children or young adults. Some worry that certain books share government secrets. Other people fear specific books go against their religion. Their concerns have led to heated debates in communities across the country.

Librarians are trapped in the middle of these efforts to censor library materials. People in their communities may become angry at them. They have faced legal charges and threats for refusing to remove books. Others, like Lesley, have lost their jobs.

Yet many librarians continue to fight for the freedom to read. They believe that libraries should be welcoming spaces where everyone can gather and learn. Former Texas librarian Suzette Baker said, "Libraries are neutral spaces. They should be protected as such. We need a free library, a library of everything, a library that reflects the good, the bad, and the ugly."

Librarian Trish Belenson organizes the bookshelves at Bella Vista Elementary School in Oakland, California.

FAMOUS BANNED BOOKS

Did you know that some of the most famous books in history have been banned at one time? Here are a few examples.

- **The Harry Potter series by J.K. Rowling:** These books were banned in some schools because people thought they promote witchcraft.
- ***The Catcher in the Rye* by J.D. Salinger:** This book was banned for its language and themes.
- ***To Kill a Mockingbird* by Harper Lee:** Some schools banned this book because it deals with racism and uses offensive language.
- ***1984* by George Orwell:** This book was banned in some countries because it criticizes government control.

These books are now considered classics. Many people believe they are important to read because they make us think about important ideas.

Classics like To Kill a Mockingbird *by Harper Lee have been subject to book bans.*

Some libraries and bookstores create tables specifically to feature books that have been banned.

The battle is not just happening in libraries. Schools are also being told to remove certain books from their shelves and classrooms. A school district in Florida pulled 1,600 books from library shelves to review them for possible banning. They even reviewed dictionaries and encyclopedias. In many towns, teachers are worried about which books they can use to teach their students. People are fighting over what books should be available. They are also disagreeing about who gets to decide.

BOOK BANS THAT WERE OVERTURNED

Sometimes when people try to ban a book, others fight back and win. Here are some famous examples.

- ***The Absolutely True Diary of a Part-Time Indian* by Sherman Alexie**: This book was banned in a Washington school district in 2011 for its language and sexual content. But when school board members read the entire book themselves, they reversed their decision.
- ***And Tango Makes Three* by Justin Richardson and Peter Parnell:** This picture book tells a true story about two male penguins raising a chick together. It was banned in many places. But in 2006, after parents in Missouri challenged the ban, the book was put back on library shelves.
- ***The Bluest Eye* by Toni Morrison:** This book was banned in a Colorado school district in 2013 because it contained themes of race and incest. But students, teachers, and community members spoke out. The school board voted to keep the book in high school libraries.
- ***The Perks of Being a Wallflower* by Stephen Chbosky:** This book was banned in a Chicago suburb in 2013. It has themes of depression and mental illness. But after a student petition and lots of media attention, the school board lifted the ban.

What Exactly Is a Book Ban?

A book ban is when a group or individual tries to stop other people from reading a certain book or books. In the United States, this may mean a school won't let students read a particular book. A library might remove a book from its shelves. Other countries can be even more strict with book bans. Some governments make it against the law to own or read certain books.

There are different types of book bans in the United States. Sometimes a book is completely removed from a library or school. A 2022 Missouri law against sexual content forced school libraries

Mark Twain's Adventures of Huckleberry Finn *has been included on book ban lists over the years.*

to remove almost 300 titles from their shelves. These included titles by Mark Twain and William Shakespeare, books about the Holocaust, and even *The Children's Bible*. A book might not be removed altogether. It could be put in a special section where kids can't get to it without permission from a parent or guardian.

Sometimes books are banned only for certain age groups. The fear is that these books contain ideas kids are not yet ready to understand. The book *T.E. Lawrence (Lives of Notable Gay Men and Lesbians)* by Daniel Wolfe was removed from the Anaheim California School District because school officials said the book was too mature for middle school students.

Books that get banned often have one or more of the following characteristics.

- They are written by an author of color.
- They are about LGBTQIA+ people and topics.
- They talk about difficult parts of history.

The Hate U Give by Angie Thomas talks about racism and police violence. It was one of the top ten most banned books in the United States for many years. Young adult fiction author Ellen Hopkins writes about sensitive topics including drug use and human trafficking. In 2023 fifty-two US school districts removed nineteen titles by Hopkins from their shelves.

Angie Thomas signs copies of her bestselling novel The Hate U Give *in 2018.*

Just because someone challenges a book doesn't mean it will necessarily be banned. Libraries and schools have processes to review challenged books. They consider things such as how well the book is written, its appropriateness for different age groups, and its overall value to readers.

Fear of Ideas

While book bans have become more common, they are not a new concept. Limiting access to ideas and books has been around for thousands of years. It began almost as soon as people started writing.

The first evidence of writing came from Sumer about 5,000 years ago. (Sumer was a country located between the Tigris and Euphrates Rivers. It is now part of southern Iraq.) These early writings were mostly about practical things, such as keeping track of crops and trade. As writing developed, people began sharing personal stories, beliefs, and ideas.

By 500 BCE, people were writing on paper scrolls by hand. This made it easier to share ideas over long distances. But it also meant that political rulers could try to control which ideas were allowed to spread.

Early writings discovered at an excavation site in Tello, Iraq (which was once Sumer)

One of the earliest known book burnings was in 213 BCE. A Chinese emperor named Qin Shi Huang ordered all the books in his kingdom be burned. He was afraid that people would read about past emperors and compare them to him. He even had scholars buried alive for hiding books.

Chinese emperor Qin Shi Huang

Politicians in ancient Rome would sometimes ban books that they thought were dangerous. The Roman poet Ovid wrote a book called *Ars Amatoria* (*The Art of Love*). It was banned by the emperor Augustus in the year 8. Ovid's book discussed adultery. This is when a married person has sex with someone other than their spouse. Roman law made adultery illegal. *Ars Amatoria* was banned for being immoral. Ovid was also banished from Rome.

One famous person who burned books was a priest named Girolamo Savonarola. In 1497 in Florence, Italy, he held a big bonfire. He burned books, art, and other things he thought were sinful. This event was called a "bonfire of the vanities."

A rendering of the "bonfire of the vanities" in fifteenth-century Florence, Italy

During the Middle Ages in Europe, the Catholic Church had control over which books people could read. They made a list called Index Librorum Prohibitorum. In English, this translates to "Index of Forbidden Books." It listed all the books people were forbidden to read. This list existed for over 400 years, from 1559 to 1966.

Even religious texts weren't safe from banning. In 1524 a scholar named William Tyndale translated the New Testament of the Bible from Latin into English. This was against the law at the time and thousands of copies were burned. Tyndale was eventually executed for his translation work. Many people thought it was dangerous for people to be able to read (and interpret) the Bible for themselves.

In 1642 the English government said that plays could no longer be performed in theaters. The works of William Shakespeare and other playwrights were banned by the Puritans (a religious group that wanted to change society). They thought that the plays were too comical and sexual. Theaters were closed or used for other events for eighteen years.

Mr. WILLIAM
SHAKESPEARES
COMEDIES,
HISTORIES, &
TRAGEDIES.
Publiſhed according to the True Originall Copies.

LONDON
Printed by Iſaac Iaggard, and Ed. Blount. 1623.

William Shakespeare was subject to book bans.

In the 1600s, the famous scientist Galileo Galilei was ordered to a lifetime of house arrest for writing that Earth moved around the sun. The belief at the time was that the sun moved around Earth. His writings were banned by the Catholic Church. His ideas went against what they believed.

Throughout history many people have been afraid of new or different ideas. Some have tried to control what others read or think. But despite these efforts, new ideas have a way of spreading. Books that were banned are now considered classics. And ideas that were once thought to be radical and dangerous are now common knowledge.

When Governments Step In

Sometimes entire countries ban books. This is often because the government is afraid of certain ideas challenging their own. The government may fear that these books will make people do dangerous or illegal things.

In the United States, the first known book ban occurred in 1637. A lawyer named Thomas Morton wrote a book called *The New English Canaan*. A section of the book described the settlers' poor treatment of Native Americans. The Puritans banned the book and arrested Morton.

In 1744 Germany's government banned books by writer Johann Wolfgang von Goethe. Goethe wrote a book called *The Sorrows of Young Werther*. It told the story of a young man who kills himself because of unrequited love. The government was worried that the book would encourage young people to commit suicide.

In 1807 France banned books by the author Marquis de Sade. De Sade wrote books with a lot of sexual content. Many people found them shocking. His son asked authorities to burn all his father's books after he passed away in 1814.

During the Civil War (1861–1865) in the United States, many book bans were related to slavery. By the 1850s, some states had outlawed all antislavery writing. In 1851 author Harriet Beecher Stowe ignored these laws. She published *Uncle Tom's Cabin*, a novel about the evils of slavery. The book was publicly burned and banned by slaveholders in Southern states.

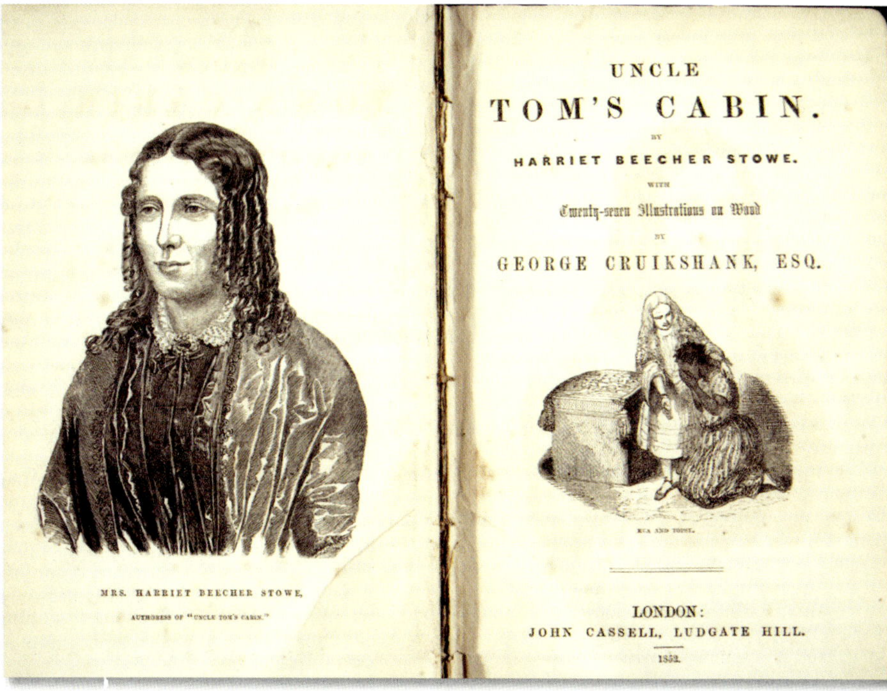

When it was released in the 1850s, Harriet Beecher Stowe's* Uncle Tom's Cabin *was quickly banned.

On the Origin of Species by Charles Darwin was one of the most controversial books ever written. First published in 1859, the book's subject matter went against religious beliefs about the origins of life on Earth. It was immediately banned by the library of Trinity College, Cambridge, where Darwin had been a student.

In 1925 the State of Tennessee banned the teaching of Darwin's theories in its schools. That law remained in place until 1967. *On the Origin of Species* was also banned in Yugoslavia in 1935 and in Greece in 1937. Even today some people try to keep this book out of schools.

Charles Darwin's book On the Origin of Species *disputed the origins of life on Earth.*

Even famous books now considered classics have been banned in different countries. In 1929 the Sherlock Holmes stories by Arthur Conan Doyle were banned in the Soviet Union (a former nation made up of fifteen republics). The government thought the stories talked too much about the supernatural. *Call of the Wild* by Jack London was banned in Italy and Yugoslavia under fascist governments who disliked the author's socialist ideas. *Alice's Adventures in Wonderland* by Lewis Carroll was banned in China in 1931. The governor of Hunan thought it was insulting to have animal characters talk like humans.

WHY ARE CHILDREN'S BOOKS BANNED MORE OFTEN?

Children's books are banned more often than books for adults. Here's why.

- **Protection:** Many adults think they need to protect kids from certain ideas or information. They worry that some books might be too scary, violent, or mature for young readers.
- **Controversial topics:** Some children's books talk about things such as racism, gender identity, or sexuality. Some adults think kids aren't ready for these topics yet.
- **School libraries:** Most book bans happen in schools. Since kids spend a lot of time at school, there's more focus on what books are available there.
- **Parental concern:** Parents often have strong opinions about what their kids should read. They might challenge books they think are inappropriate.
- **Illustrations:** Picture books can be targets because their images might be considered inappropriate, even if the text isn't.

Many people believe that kids should have access to a wide range of books. They think reading different kinds of stories helps children learn about the world and understand others better. Others disagree. This is one reason book bans are still debated today.

The works of visionary physicist Albert Einstein were among those burned and banned in Nazi Germany.

One of the most infamous book bans in history happened in Nazi Germany in May 1933. The Nazi government held huge book burnings where they destroyed thousands of books. They banned books by Jewish authors such as Albert Einstein and Sigmund Freud. They also burned books about democracy and any books that went against their ideas.

More recently, books have been banned for various reasons. Here are just a few examples.

- Some books have been banned for "treasonous" reasons, meaning the government thought they revealed too many secrets. Examples include *The CIA and the Cult of Intelligence* and *Operation Dark Heart*. They were both banned in the 1970s.
- Other books have been banned for "moral" reasons. For example, *Slaughterhouse-Five* by Kurt Vonnegut has been banned many times because some people think it's too violent and has obscene language.

- Some books are banned for religious reasons. *The Satanic Verses* by Salman Rushdie was banned in Bangladesh, India, Sri Lanka, Sudan, and other countries. Some people thought it was disrespectful to Islam. In the late 1980s, the book caused violent protests and attacks on bookstores all over the world. Rushdie was forced into hiding where he wrote under a different name.

In Ireland the Censorship of Publications Board banned books throughout the twentieth century by famous authors such as John Steinbeck and F. Scott Fitzgerald. The board still exists but is no longer functioning. It hasn't banned any more books since 2016. In 2023 members of the Irish government began discussing ending the board.

Historian Aoife Bhreatnach told Ireland's national news service, RTÉ, "There are very few records from this office of its daily workings. It's a tradition that censorship tries to erase itself, and tries to make itself invisible, and that's very much how the Irish office operated." Many people argue that governments shouldn't have this kind of control over what people read.

Censorship

Censorship is when someone tries to stop others from seeing, hearing, or expressing certain ideas. It does not apply to just books. Censorship can affect movies, music, art, and even what people say online.

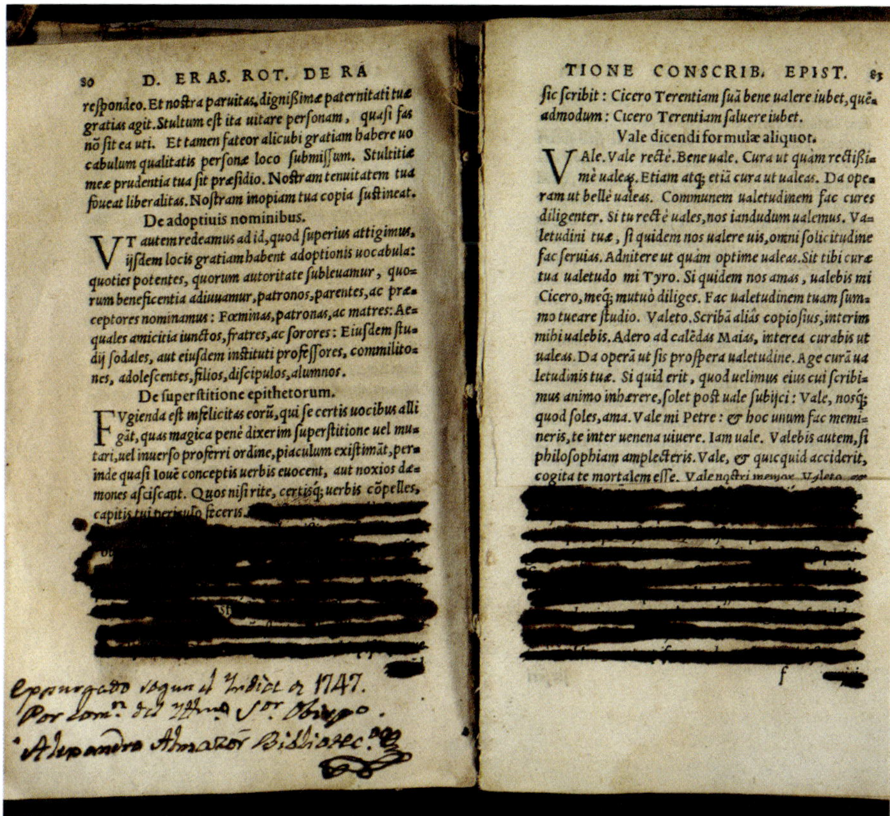

80 D. ERAS. ROT. DE RA

reſpondeo. Et noſtra paruitas, digniſſimæ paternitati tuæ gratias agit. Stultum eſt ita uitare perſonam, quaſi fas nõ ſit ea uti. Et tamen fateor alicubi gratiam habere uocabulum qualitatis perſonæ loco ſubmiſſum. Stultitiæ meæ prudentia tua ſit præſidio. Noſtram tenuitatem tua foueat liberalitas. Noſtram inopiam tua copia ſuſtineat.

De adoptiuis nominibus.

VT autem redeamus ad id, quod ſuperius attigimus, iiſdem locis gratiam habent adoptionis uocabula: quoties potentes, quorum autoritate ſubleuamur, quorum beneficentia adiuuamur, patronos, parentes, ac præceptores nominamus: Fœminas, patronas, ac matres: Aequales amicitia iunctos, fratres, ac ſorores: Eiuſdem ſtudii ſodales, aut eiuſdem inſtituti profeſſores, commilitones, adoleſcentes, filios, diſcipulos, alumnos.

De ſuperſtitione epithetorum.

FVgienda eſt infelicitas eorũ, qui ſe certis uocibus alligãt, quas magica pene dixerim ſuperſtitione uel mutari, uel inuerſo proferri ordine, piaculum exiſtimãt, perinde quaſi Iouẽ conceptis uerbis euocent, aut noxios dæmones aſciſcant. Quos niſi rite, certiſq; uerbis cõpelles, capitis tui periculo feceris.

TIONE CONSCRIB. EPIST. 83

ſic ſcribit: Cicero Terentiam ſuã bene ualere iubet, quẽadmodum: Cicero Terentiam ſaluere iubet.

Vale dicendi formulæ aliquot.

VAle. Vale rectè. Bene uale. Cura ut quàm rectiſſimè ualeas. Etiam atq; etiã cura ut ualeas. Da operam ut bellè ualeas. Communem ualetudinem fac cures diligenter. Si tu rectè uales, nos iandudum ualemus. Valetudini tuæ, ſi quidem nos ualere uis, omni ſolicitudine fac ſeruias. Adnitere ut quàm optime ualeas. Sit tibi curæ tua ualetudo mi Tyro. Si quidem nos amas, ualebis mi Cicero, meq; mutuò diliges. Fac ualetudinem tuam ſummo tueare ſtudio. Valeto. Scribã aliàs copioſius, interim mihi ualebis. Adero ad calẽdas Maias, interea curabis ut ualeas. Da operã ut ſis proſpera ualetudine. Age curã ualetudinis tuæ. Si quid erit, quod uelimus eius cui ſcribimus animo inhærere, ſolet poſt uale ſubiici: Vale, noſq; quod ſoles, ama. Vale mi Petre: & hoc unum fac memineris, te inter uenena uiuere. Iam uale. Valebis autem, ſi philoſophiam amplecteris. Vale, & quicquid acciderit, cogita te mortalem eſſe.

Censored pages in a book

There's a long history of censorship around the world. In ancient Greece, Socrates was executed for his ideas and for "corrupting the youth" with his teachings. In medieval Europe, the Catholic Church censored many scientific ideas that went against their beliefs. During World War II (1939–1945), many countries censored news about the war to keep up morale and hide information from enemies.

In certain instances, some people think that censorship can be good. They believe it can protect national security by safeguarding secrets. They claim it can keep people safe from dangerous ideas. They think it protects children from content that's not appropriate for them. And they claim censorship can be used to stop the spread of false information.

Some people argue that books like *The Anarchist Cookbook*, which contains instructions for making explosives, should be censored. They believe the information could be dangerous if it is misused. Others think censorship is wrong. They believe everyone should be free to share their ideas, even if others don't agree with them.

People may argue that censorship goes against our right to freedom of speech. They believe it can be used to control people and hide the truth. Some claim it prevents new ideas from spreading. People who oppose censorship think that everyone should be able to decide for themselves what they want to read.

In the United States, the First Amendment to the Constitution protects freedom of speech and press. This means the government can't censor most forms of expression, including books. The First Amendment protects all of the following.

- Ideas, even if they're unpopular
- Art, including books, movies, and music
- Personal expression, such as the clothes you wear or the signs you carry at a protest

HOW TO FIGHT BOOK BANS

If you want to help fight book bans, there are many things you can do.

- **Read Banned Books: The more people who read these books, the harder it is to keep them away from others.**
- **Talk About It: Discuss banned books with your friends, family, and teachers. Explain why you think it's important for everyone to have access to different ideas.**
- **Join a Banned Book Club: Some schools and libraries have clubs where people read and discuss banned books.**
- **Write Letters: If a book is being challenged in your school or library, write a letter to the school board or library director explaining why the book should stay.**
- **Stay Informed: Keep up with news about book bans and censorship. Organizations such as the ALA and PEN America provide updates and resources.**

But the First Amendment doesn't protect everything. Here are some things it doesn't protect.

- Obscenity (things that are considered too rude or gross by community standards)
- Child pornography
- Defamation (lies that hurt someone's reputation)

Congress of the United States

The Bill of Rights is part of the United States Constitution.

- False advertising
- True threats of violence
- Speech that's likely to cause immediate violence

Even with these protections, there are still debates about censorship in the United States. Some people argue that certain books should be removed from school libraries because they're not appropriate for kids. Others say this is a form of censorship and that kids should have access to a wide range of books.

The internet has created new challenges for censorship. It's much harder to control information online, but some countries try. China has a "Great Firewall" that blocks many websites and controls what Chinese citizens can see online.

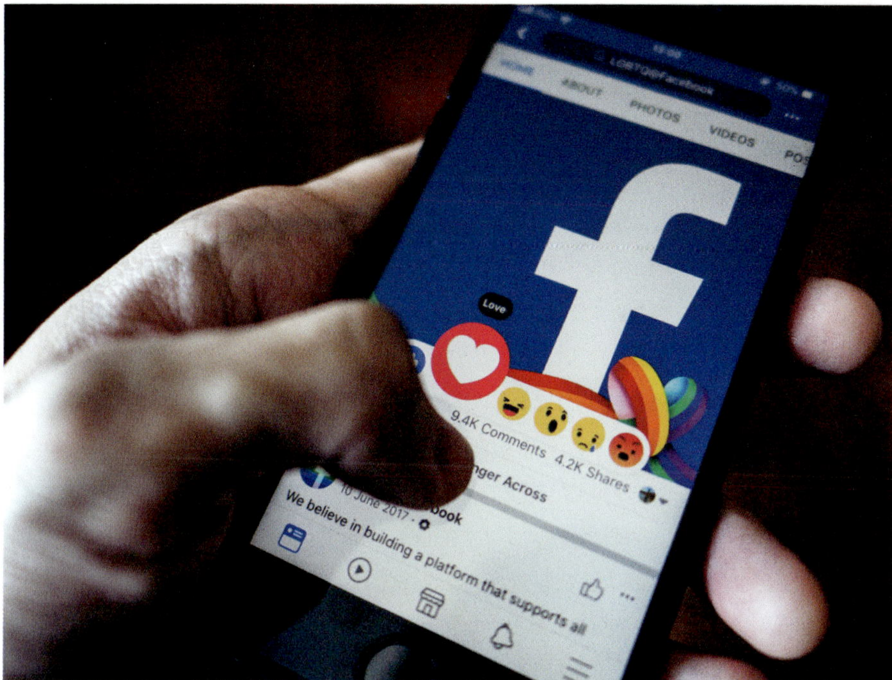

Facebook and other social media platforms have faced censorship.

Social media platforms such as Facebook and X (formerly Twitter) also face decisions about what content to allow. When they remove posts or ban users, some people call this censorship. Others say private companies have the right to set their own rules.

Censorship is a complex issue with no easy answers. It involves balancing different rights and values, such as freedom of expression, public safety, and protecting vulnerable people. As our world becomes more connected, debates about censorship are likely to continue.

Books at Libraries vs. Books at Schools

There's often a difference between the books you find on the shelves of a public library and the books in school libraries and classrooms. This is because schools need to consider what's appropriate for students of different ages. They also deal with parents who have concerns about what their children are reading.

John Scopes was arrested for teaching Darwin's theory of evolution to high school students.

One of the most famous cases about books in schools happened in 1925. A teacher named John Scopes was arrested for teaching evolution in his science class. At that time, it was against the law in Tennessee to teach anything that denied the Biblical story of human creation.

"Education means broadening. . . . If you limit a teacher to only one side of anything the whole country will eventually have only one thought, be one individual," Scopes explained. "I believe in teaching every aspect of every problem or theory." Scopes was found guilty and fined $100. This trial brought national attention to the debate over what should be taught in schools.

There are still debates about what books should be in schools. Some parents are concerned about books that address sensitive topics such as sex, violence, drug use, and racism and other forms of discrimination, as well as religious or political ideas. When parents or community members don't like a book being taught at school, they might challenge it. This means they ask for the book to be removed or moved somewhere that makes it harder to find and borrow.

Schools usually have a process for reviewing these challenges. They might decide to do any of the following.

- Keep the book where it is
- Move it to a different grade level
- Require parent or guardian permission for students to read it
- Remove the book entirely

However, school boards and administrators can't just ban any book. The First Amendment still applies to schools. In 1982 there was an important Supreme Court case called *Board of Education, Island Trees Union Free School District No. 26 v. Pico* (*Board of Education v. Pico* for short). The Court ruled that school officials can't remove books from school libraries just because they disagree with the ideas in those books.

HOW BOOK BANS AFFECT STUDENTS' MENTAL HEALTH AND WELL-BEING

Book bans don't just limit what students can read. They can also impact their mental health and well-being. Here are some mental-health impacts that book bans may have.

- **Feeling Excluded:** When books about certain groups such as LGBTQIA+ people or people of color are banned, students from those groups might feel as if their experiences aren't important or valid. This can lead to feelings of exclusion and isolation.
- **Limiting Understanding:** Books help us understand different perspectives and experiences. When students can't read about people who are different than they are, it can limit their understanding and empathy.
- **Stress and Anxiety:** The controversy around book bans can create a stressful environment for students. They might worry about what they can and can't read. They may feel anxious about the debates happening around them.
- **Impact on Learning:** Reading a variety of books is important for learning. When books are banned, it can limit students' access to diverse ideas and information, which can impact their education.
- **Censorship:** Knowing that certain books are banned can make students feel as if their freedom to explore and learn is being restricted. This can discourage them from seeking out new information and ideas.

So how do schools decide which books are allowed? They usually consider some or all of the following.

- The educational value of the book
- Whether it's appropriate for the age of the students
- How well it fits with the curriculum
- Community standards and values

Sometimes, state laws can affect what books are allowed in schools. Several states have passed laws that limit how topics such as race, sexuality, and gender can be taught. These laws can make it harder for teachers to use certain books in their classes.

Minnesota mother Tammy Aaberg addresses the school board about its policies concerning LGBTQIA+ issues in the curriculum.

The debate over books in schools is often heated because it involves questions about education, parental rights, and freedom of speech. Some people think schools should expose students to a wide range of ideas, even if they're controversial. Others believe schools should stick to "safe" topics and leave more sensitive subjects for families to discuss at home.

In recent years, there have been more challenges to books in schools. This has led to intense debates in many communities about what students should be reading and learning about in school. Florida had the highest number of school library book bans in 2023. New state laws designed to regulate reading materials made this possible.

PEN America CEO Suzanne Nossel speaks to an audience in May 2024.

"In some ways, what's happening in Florida is incubated and then spread nationwide," Kasey Meehan, the program director of PEN America's Freedom to Read Program, told the *New York Times*. "We see the way in which very harmful pieces of legislation that have led to so much of the book banning crisis in Florida have been replicated, or provisions of those laws have been proposed or enacted in states like South Carolina and Iowa and Idaho."

Legal Loopholes

The First Amendment protects free speech, but there are some exceptions. Legal loopholes allow for certain types of book bans, even in schools. Here's how these loopholes work.

- Obscenity: Books can be banned from schools if they're considered obscene. Obscenity usually means offensive, rude, or shocking. The problem is that the definition of obscenity can vary from community to community. People have different opinions about which words and images are obscene.
- Age-appropriateness: Courts are more likely to accept rules limiting school libraries to age-appropriate materials. This gives schools some flexibility in limiting access to certain books for younger students.
- Community standards: School boards oversee all school business, including library collections. They often make decisions based on community values, which can lead to book removals.
- Review processes: Many book bans start as bans pending investigation. Books can be removed from shelves during a review process. This process may take months or even a full school year.

- State laws: Some states have passed laws that restrict teaching about certain topics such as race, gender, or LGBTQIA+ issues. These laws can lead to book bans.

The 1982 Supreme Court case *Board of Education v. Pico* did not create any laws about book bans. The Court's decision is not entirely clear. It ruled that school boards get to decide which books can be in libraries. But those decisions can't violate the First Amendment. This vague ruling has left room for ongoing debates and legal challenges.

Florida teacher Michael Woods stands in front of his high school's sign in protest of Governor Ron DeSantis's decision to allow book bans.

Children's book* And Tango Makes Three *raised concerns over its theme of two male penguins raising a baby chick.

Pushing Back against Bans

Despite the rise in book bans, many individuals and organizations are fighting back. Action is needed, especially by certain groups.

1. Librarians on the front lines: Many librarians are risking their jobs to protect intellectual freedom. Some, such as Suzette Baker in Texas, have even filed lawsuits after being fired for refusing to remove books or for organizing educational programs around topics such as race and LGBTQIA+ issues.

2. Legal action: Organizations such as the American Civil Liberties Union (ACLU) are filing lawsuits to challenge book bans and defend the right to read.
3. Banned Books Week: This annual event, sponsored by the ALA and other organizations, celebrates the freedom to read and draws attention to banned books.
4. State legislation: Some states are pushing back against book bans. Minnesota, Washington, Maryland, Illinois, and several other states have passed laws making it illegal for libraries to remove books based on the ideas they contain.
5. Education and awareness: Organizations such as PEN America are tracking book bans and educating people about their impact on free expression and education.
6. Community involvement: Many parents, students, and community members are speaking out at school board meetings. Some also organize protests to protect the books in their local libraries.
7. Alternative access: Some groups are creating banned book clubs or setting up free libraries with banned books to ensure access to these materials.
8. Author involvement: Many authors of banned books are speaking out, giving interviews, and publishing articles defending their work.

The fight against banning books is ongoing. New challenges are always arising. But many people are working hard to protect the right to read. They are making sure that different voices and stories are available in schools and libraries all over the country—and even the world.

Important Dates

212 BCE	Chinese emperor Qin Shi Huang orders all the books in his kingdom be burned.
8	Ovid's *Ars Amatoria (The Art of Love)* is banned by the emperor Augustus.
1497	Priest Girolamo Savonarola burns books he finds sinful in a "bonfire of the vanities."
1559	The first Index Librorum Prohibitorum is published.
1633	The Roman Catholic Church bans Galileo's writings.
1637	*New English Canaan* by Thomas Morton becomes the first book to be banned in the United States.
1744	The German government bans Johann Wolfgang von Goethe's book *The Sorrows of Young Werther.*
1851	Harriet Beecher Stowe's antislavery novel *Uncle Tom's Cabin* is published, then banned by slaveholders in Southern states.

1925	The trial of Tennessee teacher John Scopes begins.
1933	The Nazi party burns thousands of books written by Jewish authors.
1982	The US Supreme Court rules on *Board of Education v. Pico*, one of the only cases the Court has heard related to book bans. Banned Books Week is established.
1988	*The Satanic Verses* by Salman Rushdie is published, then banned in many countries.
2005	Picture book *And Tango Makes Three* is published. It was the most challenged book in public schools and libraries in 2006, 2007, 2008, and 2010.
2023	Wyoming librarian Terri Lesley is fired from her job for refusing to remove books about LGBTQIA+ topics from her library's collection.
2024	PEN America reports a surge in book bans for the last half of 2023 with 4,349 instances across twenty-three states and fifty-two public school districts.

Source Notes

7 Natalie Batiste, “A Wyoming Public Library Board Fired Its Head Librarian after She Refused to Remove Books,” Huffpost.com, August 15, 2023, https://www.huffpost.com/entry/librarian-fired-wyoming books_n_64da5ab9e4b08e55c4cd8325.

10 Casey Kuhn, “Attempts to Ban Books Are at an All-Time High. These Librarians Are Fighting Back,” *PBS NewsHour*, April 11, 2024, https://www.pbs.org/newshour/arts/attempts-to-ban-books-are-at-an-all-time-high-these-librarians-are-fighting-back.

26 Aoife Ryan-Christensen, “Why Ireland Banned over 12,000 ‘Evil’ and ‘Unwholesome’ Books,” RTE, August 2, 2024, https://www.rte.ie/brainstorm/2024/0802/1463072-ireland-banned-books-censorship-of-publications-board-committee-on-evil-literature-/.

32–33 “John Scopes,” UMKC School of Law, 2024, https://law2.umkc.edu/faculty/projects/ftrials/scopes/Sco_sco.htm#:~:text=Scopes%20also%20spoke.

36–37 Alexandra Alter, “Book Bans Continue to Surge in Public Schools,” *New York Times*, April 16, 2024, https://www.nytimes.com/2024/04/16/books/book-bans-public-schools.html.

Selected Bibliography

American Experience. “Books behind Bars.” PBS. September 2017. https://www.pbs.org/wgbh/americanexperience/features/books-behind-bars/.

American Library Association. “Banned Books Week: Banned Books.” https://www.ala.org/bbooks/banned.

Freedom to Read. “Bannings and Burnings in History.” 2023. https://www.freedomtoread.ca/resources/bannings-and-burnings-in-history.

Kemp, Geoff. *Censorship Moments*. New York: Bloomsbury, 2014.

Ovenden, Richard. *Burning the Books: A History of the Deliberate Destruction of Knowledge*. Cambridge, MA: Belknap Press of Harvard University, 2020.

PEN America. “Book Bans.” March 25, 2022. https://pen.org/issue/book-bans/.

Learn More

American Library Association: Get Involved
https://www.ala.org/bbooks/bannedbooksweek/ideasandresources/activity

Brightly: Banned and Challenged Books Every Teen and Tween Should Read
https://www.readbrightly.com/15-banned-books-every-tween-teen-read/

Jones, Keenan. *Angie Thomas: Hip-Hop Author and Voice of Change*. Minneapolis: Lerner Publications, 2025.

Marcus, Leonard S. *You Can't Say That! Writers for Young People Talk about Censorship, Free Expression, and the Stories They Have to Tell*. Somerville, MA: Candlewick, 2021.

National Coalition Against Censorship. *A Kids Book About Banned Books*. London: DK, 2025.

NPR—"Report: Last Year Ended with a Surge in Book Bans"
https://www.npr.org/2024/04/16/1245037718/book-bans-2023-pen-america

Index

American Civil Liberties Union (ACLU), 40
American Library Association (ALA), 8

Baker, Suzette, 10, 39
Bhreatnach, Dr. Aoife, 26
"bonfire of the vanities", 18
book burnings, 18–19, 21, 25

Campbell County Public Library, 7
censorship, 26–31, 34
Censorship of Publications Board, 26

First Amendment, 28–29, 33, 37–38

Gillette, Wyoming, 7

Huang, Qin Shi, 18

Index of Forbidden Books (Librorum Prohibitorum), 19

Lesley, Terri, 7, 9–10
LGBTQIA+, 7, 9, 15, 34, 38–39

Meehan, Kasey, 36

PEN America's Freedom to Read Program, 36

Savonarola, Girolamo, 18

Photo Acknowledgments

Images used: Mr. Satterly/Wikimedia Commons (WTF Public License), p. 6; Patti McConville/Alamy, p. 8; Paul Chinn/San Francisco Chronicle/Getty Images, p. 10; Richard Levine/Alamy, p. 11; Anthony Man/South Florida *Sun Sentinel*/TNS/Alamy, p. 12; © Nancy Kaszerman/ZUMA Press Wire/Alamy, p. 15; AP Photo/Rogelio V. Solis, p. 16; ASAAD NIAZI/AFP/Getty Images, p. 17; Wikimedia Commons PD, pp. 18, 20, 23; Michelle Bridges/Alamy, p. 19; Fine Art Images/Heritage Images/Getty Images, p. 22; Library of Congress, pp. 25, 30; PRISMA ARCHIVO/Alamy, p. 27; Wachiwit/Shutterstock, p. 31; © Hulton-Deutsch Collection/CORBIS/Corbis/Getty Images, p. 32; AP Photo/*The Star Tribune*, Renee Jones Schneider, p. 35; Jamie McCarthy/PEN America/Getty Images, p. 36; AP Photo/Jim Rassol, p. 38; AP Photo/Nam Y. Huh, p. 39. Design Elements: Golubovy/Shutterstock; MargJohnsonVA/Shutterstock; Katie Dvorak/Shutterstock; Olena Dumanchuk/Shutterstock.

Cover: MVolodymyr/Shutterstock.